DEATH IN APRIL

&

Other Poems

DEATH IN APRIL

&

Other Poems

BY

G. ROSTREVOR HAMILTON

CAMBRIDGE
AT THE UNIVERSITY PRESS
1944

CAMBRIDGE
UNIVERSITY PRESS

University Printing House, Cambridge CB2 8BS, United Kingdom

Published in the United States of America by Cambridge University Press, New York

Cambridge University Press is part of the University of Cambridge.

It furthers the University's mission by disseminating knowledge in the pursuit of education, learning and research at the highest international levels of excellence.

www.cambridge.org
Information on this title: www.cambridge.org/9781107641525

© Cambridge University Press 1944

First published 1944
First paperback edition 2014

A catalogue record for this publication is available from the British Library

ISBN 978-1-107-64152-5 Paperback

TO A COMPANY OF FRIENDS
IN MEMORY OF THE 30TH NOVEMBER
1943

CONTENTS

Most of these poems have appeared in *The Abinger Chronicle*, *Country Life*, *English*, *The Fortnightly Review*, *The Guardian*, *Kingdom Come*, *The Listener*, *The National Review*, *The New English Weekly*, *The Nineteenth Century*, *The Observer*, *The Poetry Review*, *The Sunday Times*, *The Times*, and *The Times Literary Supplement*. I thank the several editors for permission to reprint.

G. R. H.

THE RUNNER

'*Within the enchanted region of the Renaissance.*'   PATER.
'*In depraved May.*'   T.S.ELIOT, *Gerontion.*

I saw him, the Runner,
As in a bee-line he flew,
Threw
No look over shoulder, driven feet
Regular as quick heart-beat
Hitting the dust.   Behind
Only a blindness of hair,
As hands clutched air,
Pointed the wind;
Before, from the thin face, forward strained wan,
Eyes' sharp-lit jewels shone.

Breathing hard, the Runner,
The Runner cried,
I run, Lord, to Thy side;
Earth have denied,
Love not, he cried:
Violence, vanity, lust
Flee from, he cried,
Thee only trust;
Avoiding all would be free,
Joined only, he cried, to Thee.

My son (I seemed that Runner then,
I, derelict of men),
My son (the gentle voice replied
Of Him I saw not), O My son,

Would you in such great haste
The creature shun,
To the Creator run?
Offer a green distaste,
And sacrifice
Things loveless, of low price?
In Me escape
From things of human, and of natural, shape?
What! does your sonhood think
I, even I, eternally who yearn
With love for the bridal earth, can break the link
That handfasts Me, as easily as you,
Who do not love, can do?

My son, since you would be
Truly My son, and joined to Me,
First shall your soul, your senses, have re-birth,
And learn, apart from Me, the love of earth;
Your eyes mark beauty, and your ears
Be slaked with singing of sweet choristers;
Your mouth taste honey, and your mind
Delight in conversation with its kind;
Mortal, contented scan
The arts and mortal monuments of man;
Even in corruption see—
As the white grass that waves
On sullen marshes, over sunken graves,—
A fair vitality;
So pleasured and so parted from My side,
So on the swell and sparkle of the tide
That, were it not
For that light under-tow of the great sea
That pulls your heart to Me,
You might rest happy and all else forgot.

Oh then, at height of some fair summer day,
Begin, in winter grief, to turn away;

Leave all your friends, a desert path pursued,
You, loving company, in solitude.
Oh then make deaf your ears; renounce your love
Of singing, seek Me through a songless grove;
Shut from your eyes the showery vision, come
At last, in voluntary blindness, home.
Oh stumbling then through anguish of that night,
Discover Me your friend, your song, your light;
Have ears to hear again, and eyes to see,
Who still must love the world, but love the world
    with Me.

I saw that Runner stand; and then re-trace
The way he ran, but at a walking pace.

PRAYER FOR THE NEW-BORN

We, midway travellers between birth and death,
Pray for the nurselings, the unknowing, the new-born,
Still sunned by their madonnas' eyes, surrounded
By shade of arm, shield of breast,
From hardness confused of lancing light,
Frown of strangeness, fright of space unbounded;

Who, not divided yet, division of flesh
Weakly assume, and billows of sound beat
Through winds of scent and colour without defining;
For whom, away from close breast,
All distances unfocused bear
Rumour of cold and menace of sound shining;

For whom, in distance of time, for whom unborn,
Through generations of dream and dark will
Drops in the swift, the tributaried river
Slid and mingled, sobbed farewell,
Heavy with vague inheritance,
Lost in the shifting years till birth deliver;

So sunk, so scattered, in general dream so old,
For them we pray, inheritors last-come
Who weep and wake in the body's strange assembling;
For the unaccustomed eye afraid
Of dazzle, the ear of noise, the hand
Waving or clasped in strain, the thin cry trembling.

For them we pray—new-come in a world unknown
That soon shall grow familiar—a long life
Happier than ours; as men pray desolate-hearted
For other travellers who go,
And slip even from Earth's breast,
Bound for an unknown world, the new-departed.

THE DISCORD

(*To the parents of* J.C.R.P.—*killed in action off Crete*)

At such an hour, when day
On the broad river makes her last delay,
And swans in that remaining brilliance rest
On luminous reflections, breast to breast,
And sway white necks like ghostly flower-stems;

At such an hour my mind,
By fever at the centre long confined,
Has spread to the circumference, has been
Circle and very conscience of the scene,
All light and silence with the silver Thames.

So fair a scene is set
This evening, with peace descending; yet,
Though the winged imminence of night alarm
And distant general battle may not harm
The ringed-in quiet, the suspense of breath,

The scene, so fair, has loss
For me of all significance—across
The gentle brightness of day's residue
There breaks discordantly the pictured blue
Mediterranean, and a boy's death.

June 1941.

BEGINNING

A hundred generations gone
  Are links of day and night for us
Since Phoebus' golden races shone
  On Homer and Herodotus.

Across the gulf of wake and sleep
  The flickering coursers from that prime
In vast acceleration leap
  To syncopate the tract of Time;

Then at this breathing moment rein
  Their speed—and lo! a creeping sun
Faces a dark, a boundless plain:
  Homer and we have scarce begun.

THE GLOBE

The world of Mind—
orbis intellectualis,
*receiving into
its depth the image
of all things;*

Singular and secret globe
Weaving images for robe,
Spinning with gradualness of light
From clear noon to hooded night,
Argus-eyed, and yet in trance
Drawing for its sustenance
Rays from spirit-regions, whose
Bright embraces round it close;
Such the Mind: with richer store
Of Capes and Indies to explore
Than the wide extremes of Earth
Before the Navigator's* birth;
Whose sea venturings, long passed,
Lie in sunken memory glassed
Where the mind's dismissal drowns
Pinnacles of earthly towns,
And the shine of earthly streams
Flows in underground of dreams.

*burying in image,
the record of pre-
history and history,*

Mind's abyss and Time's abyss;
Argus eyes, they nothing miss,
Never-closed recording eyes
Hoarding with remote surprise
Fearful apparitions vast
Through their passive mirrors cast;
Mailed Leviathans that sink
Over the horizon's brink,
Beckoning to last eclipse
Triremes, galleons, battleships;
Rank Behemoths of the prime:
Bred from fire-mist and slime
Saurians, whose ridge and crest
Rear up mountains in the West

* Henry the Navigator (1394–1460).

14

For vain suns to founder on,
Crimsoned in oblivion.
None of these, no nightmare shape
May those lidless eyes escape,
Nor at last, in dwarfish span,
The self-fronting image, Man,
Nor his struggling towers spilt
Ruinous for sand to silt;
Towers that rose, towers that fell,
To wail of voice and toll of bell
Heard no more, that yet ring deep
Smothered in smooth-chambered sleep,
Where the cymbal makes a stir
Less loud than of dulcimer,
And once thunders echo faint
In a lulled astonishment.

of the life of
Nature and the
successive works
of Man—

    Turns and turns the secret globe,
Weaving images for robe;
Ceaseless, those recording eyes
Through unwearied centuries
Intervolve with wink and glow
Of life's waving shadow-show—
Giant form and pigmy form,
Forest-lives that burst and swarm
Fevered—the expanse and wing
Of ideas self-imaging,
And immenser concepts thrown
Wild from spirit-worlds unknown.
There, successive through the dance
Mixt of gloom and radiance,
Rise, the shadows of a shade,
Fantasies of things man-made;
Wood and stone and marble there,
Zone on zone, stair on stair,
Temples, palaces of air,

Castles, campaniles, domes,
Urs and Ninevehs and Romes,
Babylons and Londons. These,
Or by swift or slow degrees,
Mime upon the fickle stage
Till death tumble them or age
Crumble, or insulting rise,
Higher to assault the skies,
Uniforms of white façades
Playing ghostly grim charades
That spell out the word Decay;
And the phantoms of to-day
Stripped of honour pass away
To sleep in darker hollows hid
Than monolith or pyramid.

buried images that
sometimes flicker
into moments of
consciousness.

    Turns the secret world, and drowns
Pinnacles of earthly towns:
Buried some, as flinty shells
Of sea-creatures through the swells
Sink, and rub the oozy floor;
Some, as when a long-shut door
Opens, and a lamp again
Shivers through the dreaming brain,
Flicker upward. So, when storm
Limns a cowering landscape's form,
Curve of hill and spire of tree
Flare in sharpened tracery,
And gold corn and grazing land
Rigid for a moment stand,
While the colour through them burns
Flame-like in translucent urns.
Over the surface stride and wheel
Vast lank images of steel,
Pylons that in death-dance rally
Skeletons across the valley,

Swift invaders seeking root
Where unquelled humilities shoot,
Where, forgetting lives long slain,
Wounds of Earth are green again.

Constant images
of the peaceful
hours and seasons;
transient and
changing images
of War;
    Falls the dew as fell the dew
When the mammoth-shape was new;
Over mountain, over dale
Swings the tumult of the gale,
As it swung when towers fell
To wail of voice and toll of bell,
Faint lost cataracts of sound
Far off echoing underground.
Still those Argus eyes receive
Flame of dawn and print of eve;
Drought and moisture, heat and cold
Still their sequences unfold;
Mirrored lawn and ploughland still,
Shining glade and shaggy hill,
Year by year resume their dress,
While to fathomless recess—
Stair on stair, zone on zone—
Man-made fantasies of stone
Historied in dream are gone.
Constant are the signs of peace,
Lowing herds and fruits' increase,
Constant are the peaceful stars
High in heaven. Restless Mars,
Often though his circuit drive
Men mad-witted to contrive
Masks more hideous of death,
Does but with a fuming breath
Sully mind's serener glass;
Where through deepening levels pass,
Small as glint of deadly flies
Cruising the sepulchral skies,

Aeroplanes, and in slow ranks
Drilled automata, squat tanks.
They, like vanished monsters drawn
In rock-caves, their likeness spawn
Shadowy-pencilled in the cell
Where Moloch and Astarte dwell,
Doomed idolatries of Hell;
While in mockery of wars
Drop the dews and shine the stars.

images of peace
perpetually renewed
and engraved in
Memory, to emerge
clear in the creation
of the single mind.

Singular and secret globe,
Weaving images for robe,
Argus eyes that still inlay
Day with night and night with day,
Beast in field with man at plough,
Song and toil and wind in bough,
And, in jewelled prospect seen,
Fresh humilities of green.
Constant images, they fall
Seasonal, rhythmical,
Layer on layer, dye on dye
Deepening as depths of sky
Turn to azure, till they trace
Forms no Lethe can efface;
From whose dim retiring-place
To the poet's conscious eye
Waiting in expectancy—
Waiting, even as meadows yearn
For Persephone's return,
Who too long has shed her bloom
Pale in dusky Pluto's room—
On some hoped-for day appear,
Drenched in light uncrinkled clear,
Time-old visions; they, submerged
Long in dream, of grossness purged,
Far more real than common sight
Stand in sharpness of delight,

Ripening to a moment's birth
The memorial fields of Earth,
While, for beauty's sheer excess,
Time, in trance, stays motionless.

NOW

Fearful traveller, not to miss
Footing, shun the starred abyss.
Fasten eyes, in Time's street,
To *Now's* rimmed torchlight at your feet;
Look not on the starred abyss.

Climber, cling to your clear ledge;
Look not from *Now's* striding edge
Down, down those chasms vast
Of breaking future, broken past;
Look not from *Now's* striding edge.

Nay, with seeing eyes you climb
Street and precipice of Time,
There and there in poised suspense
Mid sheer chasms, stars immense,
On the nightmare *Now* of Time.

THAW

O sunlit prophecy of earth new-leaved,
  O poignant rain reviving the lost years,
Fall gently on the frozen heart bereaved,
  And wake at last forgotten warmth of tears:

O lovely light, fall soft on this cold bed,
And tears, bring ache of living from the dead.

DEATH IN APRIL

Ah, you that lean over the piled-up pillows,
Look up at last!
            Out of the window see
            Light upon earth, leaf upon the tree,
And this year's April fair as every other.

Look up at last!   See golden on the willows
The catkin sway.
            Now is the time for tears,
            When April, cruellest month, her trousseau wears,
And the farm fields with cries of lambs are ringing.

Look up! look up!   For now no more he needs you
And your clear eyes.
            Unharassed lies the bed,
            Nor any moan comes from the well-loved head.
None shall take harm now from your well-earned weeping.

No more the pleased and busy sunlight heeds you
Than the quiet room:
            Whose progeny indeed
            From deathly winter grew without your heed
Up into spring; while you, each lusty morning,

Watched in the sickroom; to a whisper lowered
Your natural voice;
            With careful curtains framed
            The filtering light, and all exuberance tamed
To assist you moving on your ministrations.

Last year the snowdrop and the crocus flowered,
And this year too:
            Last year your loved one felt
            The lengthening days, the illumination spelt
In white and blue and gold of earth's renewal.

This year no more: the one long night of sleeping
Drew on apace,
        From which the sun can bring,
      His glow no life, his warmth no wakening;
Nor any difference; nor any season.

And you, meantime, the shadows closer creeping,
Listened and watched;
        Rewarded by a smile,
      Were in his company still; another while
Were leagues away from him, so far he wandered—

Without a guide wandered through network mazes
Of fitful years.
        Ah! could you step with him,
      Unravel the confused and light the dim
Pathways to you familiar, calm the uneasy

Excited breathing, loosen the fixed gazes,
Link hand in hand!
        Alas, he must alone
      Walk, a bewildered stranger, through his own
Old memories that crowd and cross and darken.

Darkness; thick darkness; yet the darkness never
Could claim him quite.
        Still was the spirit whole;
      Nor were you mocked by that winged aureole,
Utter serene of peace, joy beatific

That through discomfiture of flesh, through fever
Of the whirled brain,
        One westering hour had shone—
      Now from the height the Alpine light was gone,
Gone too the pained perplexity: the body

Lay in his likeness there, a mute deceiver.
Not *this* had been
                    Partner in lively sense,
            Far-ranging thought, godlike experience,
Ambassador of an unseen world's dominion.

So much of him, and yet so less than nothing:
So real, unreal!
                    The very Spring in spate
            Held more of him, each creature for its mate
In merest bodily pride itself adorning.

And you? Look up! Lovely is April's clothing
On hill and vale.
                    For you she spreads her wealth,
            And breathes her perfume, cruel for your health
In bland indifference this Easter morning.

LAMENT FOR THE BODY

What shall we count for loss
When the body dies?
How lovely and of value in itself!
No jewels are like eyes.

Never enough lament
The adoréd face,
The vanished contours of that rarest one,
The no more moving grace.

Perishes all we see
As the flower of grass:
The dear and worshipped honour of the flesh
Must unreturning pass.

Though, fairer yet, the child
Of a mother fair
Confront you with a teasing, transient,
Elusive look of her,

Yet mark a failure too,
Nor scorn to grieve;
No this-year's-child, as the constant violet, can
A last year's beauty thieve.

Nay, even though herself
Should in bliss excel
With robe of body far more shining-clear
The robe that you love well,

Be not ashamed to grieve
For the beauty gone,
Whose true facsimile you shall not find
In heaven, to gaze upon.

LOSS OF MEMORY

His jailor body, by some yet whole nerve,
Lets through so much of spirit as may serve
Animal needs; the rest is severed, set
Deep under, buried in an oubliette.
Buried; in vain the countenance you scan,
To find, where should be index of the man,
A classic headstone cut in faultless style,
With no inscription but a wavering smile.
The past is gone, all gone. *He* (so to call
The sad survivor from that burial)
Knows not what triumphs and defeats were his,
Delights, griefs, passions, nor what ecstasies

Of skyey ardour (once when genius burned)
Racked, starved the flesh, intemperately spurned
Sensual barriers. Cry woe the hour
When body, not forgiving, waxed in power,
And spirit lay, its former lightning spent,
In tame life-sentence of imprisonment,
Nor vengeance till that day may slacken hold
When fingers mortify and sift in mould!

Oh then, at body's death, you shall not weep,
Nor say in pious phrase, 'He falls asleep':
Oh then, dishonouring years of nothingness
Shall shrivel to a summer night and less:
Oh then at last, as the long morning breaks,
'The fire burns', you'll say, 'the sleeper wakes.'

THE DENIED

(*for* RICHARD CHURCH)

This windless day denies the storm
With darkness gone; this carven form
Denies infinitude; this breath
Delicious is, denying death;
 Yet still on every side
 Triumph the things denied,
Storm, infinitude and death.

This garden-plot denies the wild,
This man of fifty years the child;
This room with curtains, shutters, bars
And candle-light denies the stars;
 Yet still on every side
 Triumph the things denied,
Infancy, wilderness and stars.

Oh wild from this poor cage of sense
Sings out the star of innocence,
And storm and death and life belong
To one clear infinite of song;
 And still on every side
 Triumph the things denied,
And singer falters not, nor song.

CORLEY: 1902

I swim, a living ghost, against the stream,
Change this real nightmare for a waking dream;
Swim, swim against the glistening stream-line
Charioted for nineteen-thirty-nine,
Time in a head-on crash; still struggling swim
Back till the fragments of to-day grow dim;
Swim struggling back till, forty years behind
This nineteen-forty-two, I wake and find
Childhood and sunny water, then again
No water, but a green and sunny lane.

For this is *Corley Lane.* I know by heart
That bend, that slope, driving the governess-cart,
And Gipsy, stubborn pony, knows them too;
In each unchanging house I know who's who;
Here at her gate good kindly Mrs Wall
With the twisted smile will answer if I call;
Here wizened Pettifer lives, and Steeley there,
Silent, important man, the carrier,
Who from his high-wheeled cart looks grimly down
On the slow-motion road, full five miles long, to town.

To town? His plodding mare and rumbling tyres
Roll on to *Coventry*, city of spires,

Ribbons and bicycles, where Peeping Tom*
Hopes the white shade Godiva still may come.
But we, we Rectory children, jog between
High-towering elms and hedge-topped walls of green,
Where only eyebright from the grassy steep
And cuckoo-flower and straggling stitchwort peep,
And no romances out of yesterday
But only White Leghorns unghostly stray.
They, the daft birds, too dignified to shun
Approaching wheels, at the last moment run,
Swerving now left, now right, wings trailed before us
All helter-skelter in an outraged chorus,
While mocking them along safe hedges flit
The chaffinch and the sideways-peering tit.
Now the lane opens; sudden on the right
Rich-sanded *Corley Rocks* come into sight,
Red Indian paradise for feet to scramble
Through lacing palisades of fern and bramble
To spots enchanted where the kettle sings
On Saturdays, and people sit in rings—
Haven of picnic, where soiled paper-bags
Still hang mid hawthorn-twigs their tell-tale flags.

Soon we are heading for home at a brisker pace,
Stable and tea-time calling. On we race
As Gipsy breaks to a canter, and the rein
Her lolloping ardour scarcely can restrain;
Down hill we swing, and up again we lurch
The last lap home, past the high-shouldered church,
To a standstill by the long brick stable. There
Old Fletcher waits us with a quizzing leer,
'You've brought her home then? Or did she bring you?'
We know him far too well to argue who—
So kind a man, we humour him with ease,
And only kinder, if we let him tease

* His effigy, looking from a window.

And laugh at his quick wit. We wave, and run
Through kitchen-garden preening in the sun,
By apple-orchard and by springy moss
Edging the velvet croquet-lawn, across
To the grey Rectory, whose brooding wings
Swallow and hide us, till our racketings
Ripple through corridors to fall subdued,
Mere murmurs, on the grown-up solitude.
Tea in the nursery: ravening we cram
The duty butter and rewarding jam,
Then soon as done, are off, with quick-said grace,
Feet fidgeting for any other place.

And many places lure us in the bound,
So wide a pleasance, of the Rectory ground.
The drive, pale pebbly river, swirls between
A shaggy hayfield and the fresh-cut green,
Banded with silver, of trim lawns that ride
Down to a hidden curve. On that smooth side
Prodigious rhododendron-clumps their bold
Bonnets of crimson from dark mounds unfold,
And fir-like, small, uncandled Christmas-trees
Stiffen in glaucous sprays. How unlike these,—
Disdaining by such uniform to please,—
The busy deserts of the hayfield spread!
Here dragon-flies their thin bright needles thread
Zigzagging; here, through breathless afternoon
Flicker the Blues, and float the Whites, and swoon
The flopping Meadow Browns; here to the skies
Two single trees in turbaned grandeur rise,
High sovereigns, each recognising each,
Cool tulip-tree and dark-bright copper beech—
Pride of the village, set within whose frame
A *Warwick* landscape turns midsummer flame
To catlike drowsiness.
                              And still between
The shaggy hayfield and the shaven green

Blinking in heat the gravel drive descends
Till shadow-chilled under tall trees it bends.
Trees overhang the highroad. Outward swing
Trees in a portly round enveloping
Garden and orchard, trees that nod and talk
Above the path nicknamed *The Lovers' Walk*,
Where on a moonlit night behind you creep
The clammy-fingered ghosts that cannot sleep.
Yet there, when night and whisperings are gone,
In friendly daylight you may walk alone,
Or in the shine of dew, as birdsongs wake,
With feet unfollowed through the circle break
And cross by open fields to *Corley Wood*:
A name by some for foxes understood,
By some for bluebells, but much more by one
For Orange Underwings that in the sun—
He droops his net, the chase not yet begun—
Fly among catkins high above the cool
Rim of a private, cloud-reflecting pool.

But that was April morning; now 'tis June,
And after tea-time. Hark! the ringing tune,
Again, of Father's axe! And Mother stands
To watch him in his shirt-sleeves with gloved hands
Chop the low trailing boughs, to make a new
Tunnel through leaves, an open-window view
To *Coventry*. Ah! there, this very minute,
The thinning space falls clear and, sharpened in it,
Three pencil spires in the showering light
Salute us, rising level* with our sight;
While, strange to think, three hundred feet below
Invisible but large as life there go
Hiscock the chemist, Moore of *The King's Head*,
Laxton and Blythe. Among the trams they tread,

* The top of St Michael's spire was said to be on a level with the
keyhole of the Rectory front-door.

28

Between the houses that lie safe and snug
As any rich man tucked up in a rug,
The centre round which all of England lies
And drinks in peace from wide, unpeopled skies.

YOUTH REMEMBERED

Wise men have set for fairest end of learning,
Feverish youth gone by,
　　To know, beyond the coloured play of sense,
　　The single whiteness of intransience,
The pearl of Truth all other pearls outpricing.

Yet how shall I not grieve that, past renewal,
My morning-time is fled?
　　What universal vision could atone—
　　Ecstatic mind 'alone with the Alone'—
For small particular raptures, day-sufficing?

Briefly my morning—in its upland valley
A stream that loitered long,
　　With time at standstill under heathered slopes,
　　Then wider, quickening with seaward hopes,
Flowed through warm-scented banks and flowers
　　enticing—

Briefly my morning passed. The silver moment
Shining to Lethe slipped:
　　And yet what foolish flashings I recall!
　　The day that I was Caesar, conquered Gaul,
Escaping from the schoolroom undetected:

The day I saw about a lofty oak-tree,
Buoyant with pinion spread,
　　No longer gazed at in a coloured plate,
　　The mighty *Purple Emperor* hold his state,
And then, my net on clumsy pole erected,

Dashed him to common earth: the day, reluctant,
I took my father's great
        Blue-calf-bound Milton, and at random read
        Of Satan—'horror Plumed' upon his head—
And stayed, surprised and shamed by so much splendour.

And later days: sudden a gold horizon
Of liberating thought:
        An hour of friendship tested: and the shared
        Excitement of a crowd: ventures we dared
And found no longer frightening: the tender,

Stealthy approach and passionate usurpation
Of love; the close turmoil;
        The hour of wild certainty, the doubt
        With premature bravado put to rout,
The desperate joy outvaluing safe pleasure.

And quiet days; the very scent and savour
Of daily things new-felt,
        Wherewith the incidents of work or play,
        Dear home affections, a mere summer day,
This hour or that, are heightened beyond measure.

Briefly my morning. Yet those days I summon
Back from the countless dead;
        Nor do they come as pitiable shades,
        The tearful ghosts of lamentable glades,
A scorn, a mockery of life departed—

Nor do they come as spirit without body,
Bare ecstasy of mind,
        But in the warm desire-moving dress
        Of bright imaginary loveliness,
Clear-seeing, quiet-thinking, and true-hearted.

FIRST AND LAST

Clear the dawn; O touch it not
    With promise of approaching day
That soon, how soon, with altered note
    Shall threaten innocence away;
O let the moment timeless be,
Pretending an eternity.

Clear the evening, yet holds
    A memory of sorrow past,
And still the first of peace enfolds,
    Storm-linked, with the tear-bright last;
O bid the moment stay, to chime
A true epitome of time.

SPRING, IN WAR TIME

The palsied winter by our grief,
    And by our hate the barren frost:
No love of ours restores the leaf,
    Nor our delight the springtime lost.

Oh! what a siege have you withstood,
    Innocent Nature! How you break
Our stubborn engines, in the blood
    What pricking of remorse awake!

Challenge to wilderness you fling
    In this green secular campaign,
But when shall be our human Spring,
    That we may march with you again?

NATURE'S WARS

Great Mother, pitiless in field and wood,
Never by you our peace was understood.
Yet are you blest; never by you were known
Our wars, our treacheries; only your own,
That not with their worst cruelty defeat
The scent and wildness of the meadowsweet,
Nor yet imperil with their darkest wrong
The flute and freedom of a blackbird's song.

THE TIDES

Up, to be dandled on dark-bosomed earth,
Those strangers to my blood,
The green enchanted children climb to birth
At Spring's flood,
And I, a ghost with beams of eyes,
Covet them still and scrutinise.

Deep into glassy chambers I decoy
Clear-imaged bud and leaf;
Then make my breath-sweet confiture of joy,
A blameless thief:
Stealing from them what is not theirs,
Rich, but not cheating Nature's heirs.

And Nature soon, lulling these orbs to rest,
May bright and arrowy burn
Behind their sockets, lighten through my breast
And, rich in turn,
Me plunder with her golden shine,
Yet steal no virtue that is mine.

So in a ghostly traffic do we cross,
Nature and I, to gain
Some booty each, but not at other's loss,
While each in vain
The other searching with mute glance
Falls on a stone-cold countenance;

Till, secret as two foreigners who meet
High on a bridge, we smile,
Conscious that both have heard beneath our feet,
Older than Nile,
In thunderous misty depths below
The tides of generation flow.

THE IVY

The ruined coach-house overlaid
    With clouds of ivy now is gone,
That through the changing seasons made
    Fair evergreen to gaze upon;
Men hacked it down, and with it hurled
To death how various a world!

No more the thrush and blackbird there
    Shall feast on berries purple-black,
When snow yet illustrates the year
    And other food their larders lack,
Then, having wetted well their throats,
Ruffle their wings and try their notes;

There not again, in joyous May,
    Shall they bring dewy moss for nest,
Fibre and whatnot, straw and clay,
    And round the circle with their breast,
Then from the ivy's topmost crown
Bugle the golden sunset down.

And there no more, in hot July,
    Shall parent sparrows to and fro
For juicy morsels, grub and fly,
    Down the sun-warm galleries go,
The lazy groundling young to feed,
Whose chirps repeat the tale of greed.

There bees shall congregate no more
    About the umbels of late bloom,
Sticky with moisture, that upbore
    Green stars above the leafy gloom
Where, deep within, the spider's lust
Lurked in cobwebs roped with dust.

There has the barn-owl lost his perch
    Where he, profaning with no hoot
The hush as of an empty church,
    Would, like an angler taking root
Beside a willowy river-brink,
A feathered statue, watch, nor wink;

No need of line or bait to throw—
    Into the stream of night would pierce
Those orbs with golden flame aglow;
    No need of hook—those talons fierce,
Like lightning with no thunder heard,
Would strike on rustle of mouse or bird.

No more; and never more for me
    That patterning of glossy-green,
Five-pointed, dark embroidery
    Shall hold in miniature the scene
Where Life betrays her sweets and stings
By trembling leaves and whirring wings.

Nor only is the outward sense
    Cheated; from this lost ivy's bower
Would Fancy often fly far hence
    To lonely lake and battled tower,
Where ruined keep and ivied wall
Have greybeard Time for seneschal.

THE TWO SONGS

(*for* WALTER DE LA MARE)

Down from the far meridian height
   Such peace that lonely song distils,
Each tremble from its tune of light
   The air's great shining bubble fills.

The shadow of the falcon fear
   Is vanished, and the owl's soft wing
Gone with the night, bequeathing here
   A faint, a tranquil quivering.

The lark, of this new crystal birth,
   Sings on to unimpassioned skies;
And, where his nest shall be, the earth
   In fair, sweet, idle rapture lies.

But other ears, not idle, take
   His music—man, whose grieving mind
And fearful heart in tumult shake,
   A sea of darkness rough with wind;

Unknowing to those stormy waves
   The singer cries his 'Peace, be still!'
The peace all human passion craves,
   The silence of creative will.

Oh! soon shall leap the lyric word,
   In heaven be quiring notes again,
A song diviner than of bird,
   The twice-born, lovelier from pain.

Not vanished now the falcon fear,
   Nor fled with night the owl's soft wing;
Harmless, those cruelties draw near,
   In strange communion listening.

FISH OF ST TROPEZ

A picture by Vladimir Polunin

Slip, slip from time, and dip
Down, down:
Leave the tick of noisy hours
For these hushed, these glaucous bowers,
Where fish-ogres pink and slate
Bloom in mockery of date,
Nor passes time where they pass by
Gold-buttoned with lugubrious eye.

Learn that fishy curl of lip,
Drown, drown:
Pride be changed for purple sheen,
Jealousy for deep sea green,
Lidless while the leering eye
Glazes, and eternally
You cruise and cruise with scarce a flick,
A single thought gone lunatic.

THE HIDING-PLACE

This house, a tongueless ruin
      Scarred and desolate,
Is neutral as a man's skull
      To what was mean or great:
One grimace, be it brick or bone,
Is all you get from a skeleton.

And yet, if glass and curtain,
      Eye and silk of skin,
Should rustle again the anatomy,
      And life sigh within,
What would you see through flesh or stuff?—
Window and eye are blank enough.

36

No crested flame, no aura
        Down the numbered street,
Or in the sweating market-square
        Where men like cattle meet,
Points the tenement or face
Where Destiny has hiding-place.

Though lifted clear the puppet,
        Who can see the string,
Or ghostly in the Brown House
        The Player torturing
Hitler's high convulsive star,
His daemon and familiar?

In homely brow and cottage
        Who sees Joan the Maid?
Or what man, in the *agora*
        Questioned and waylaid,
In snub nose and in full lip sees
Eternal-minded Socrates?

THE RED HOUSE

The man goes out each morning and shuts the door
Of the red house;
The woman watches him move across the moor,
Opens the window, heavily sweeps the floor
Of the red house;
The early sky burns cool,
White as its white reflection in the pool
By the red house.

Across the moor is nothing human beside
But the red house;
The two who live, and the hated other who died
With none but the clouds passing when he cried
From the red house—

37

The clouds white like wool,
Thick as their thick reflection in the pool
By the red house.

The man returns each evening from the moor
To the red house;
The woman watches and waits him by the door,
And he speaks, and treads again the creaking floor
Of the red house;
And the sky is dumb like a fool,
With one white star reflected in the pool
By the red house.

URIAH

(DAVID *prophesies*)

Self-guarded, lo! on the roof, star-destined, beautiful,
One washing her limbs when evening is cool:
The rains slide and fall; along her body slips
    Light, with the eye alone conspirator,
On olive shoulder slumbering and smooth hips.

Eyes, look on her! O towered in the secret body look!
So thirst great-eyed gazelles for the water-brook.
Knows she another bed? The closer is she mine,
    Tall as a cypress, lissom Bathsheba,
Scented, coming to me with oil and wine.

O that sufficient night with her star-shining hood
Might drown to-morrow in our singing blood!
For terrible her beauty—I see the unenvied light,
    The burning long ravine, the wilderness;
Harshness of spears; a host of men who fight;

A hill shaped as a skull; and one at my decree,
Whose love I wrong, whom darkness veils from me,
Set in the forefront; who, for stealth of this night's deed,
　　From the sixth to the ninth hour, my enemy,
Innocent—or there were no peace—shall bleed.

INVOCATION

O Thou, Creator from original Chaos,
What shall we ruinous men
　　Offer Thee, war at end, for new creation
　　But chaos again, our cloudy aspiration,
Formless still as the smoke of burning cities?

Or plans, a tumult of plans, the architecture
Or Babel and dark dream—
　　We, vowed to what inveterate delusion
　　That leavens Truth, near whole, with vast
　　　　confusion
Moving to laughter and tears the heavenly Pities?

Oh brood on our good-will, Thou only goodness!
Redeem our faith, our hope
　　From vanity! Engrave upon our vision
　　The human image of divine precision,
The lovely finite, clear in limb and feature:

And lay Thy hand, Thou only master-builder,
On human hands; oh build
　　A polity, from the shaken world's commotion,
　　Larger in wisdom, worthier devotion,
And man in man's free service Thy new creature!

THE STATESMAN

Only the dreamer solitary
    For sky-mark of our hope may set
Serene above the touch of time in music
    The city we desire; and yet

For justice that Utopia,
    For mercy that Jerusalem,
The statesman only to these dying cities'
    Darkness may bring light of them.

IN FEVER

Shadow tent and naphtha glare—
    Monstrous idle droves of thought
Head to tail, black horse, white mare,
    Trace an endless oval nought;

Till a waxwork, smooth, exact,
    Plastered lock on brow oblique,
Unreality's central fact,
    Unit in the nought unique,

Clicking, clacking, steps inside,
    The Dictator of the Ring;
Swings the lash in circle wide,
    Swifter makes the horses swing.

Faster, faster, the red ground
    Under frantic hooves is trod,
Merry, merry, merry-go-round,
    Worship to the waxwork god!

BIRTH

Lightest, loveliest on earth
From darkness and corruption come to birth;
Worm to its winged hour,
From dissolution the curled flower,
    And from the womb, from the dream, Helen.

Passion featureless and blind
Comes to a lucid shaping in the mind;
Grief to its carved word,
From terror of night a song heard
    Once of London, of Troy, burning.

THE WAY HOME

Eyes had no work to do; mechanical feet
Carried me home down the familiar street,
Past workmen working at the crater. Eyes
Had nothing to do, it seemed, but recognise
    The houses a full fortnight now in ruins.

Eyes had no work to do, until to-day
Ears heard from somewhere down that homeward way
A thrush at practice, note by joyous note,
And eyes looked up and saw the speckled throat
    Criss-crossed behind green swelling buds of lilac.

Then eyes had other work to do. They saw
Workmen flies in a wound with edges raw;
And a family's knobbed iron bedpost thrust
Through a still avalanche of bricks and dust;
    And a staircase carpeted with invitation.

CHISWICK

April 1941

ROOF SCENE

Beyond the leprosy of blistered wood
And writhing relic of steel where once there stood
The furniture store, two girls on a flat roof
Lie out and bask.   The sun looks down aloof
As any lordly god might look from Olympus.

Beyond again, with another ruin between,
Workmen along a higher parapet lean,
Like idlers from their cabins come on deck
To view a sail, or flotsam of a wreck,
A school of porpoise, or a rumoured island.

But now with a sudden change their backs are bent
To a tauter curve, their captured eyes intent
Where one of the girls, slow rising from her chair,
Has cast bewilderment upon the air
Of beauty hidden in light and undeciphered:

She passes by with blithe unconscious tread,
Apollo weaving a nimbus round her head;
And the cockneys stand like those who stood at gaze
From holy battlements not yet ablaze,
Forgetful of all but the passing by of Helen.

HOLBORN
June 1941

OXFORD

No cruelties of war deface your stone,
That crumbles to Time's gentleness alone;
Your wounds are in your heart, where grief and pride
Name those who loved you, and untimely died.

EPITAPHS IN GREECE

I. A GREEK SOLDIER

Go, stranger, tell the English we lie here
Servants of freedom, as our fathers were.

II. AN ENGLISH SOLDIER

Go, countryman, tell of a stranger's pride,
Who shared your heritage and served and died.

III. AN AUSTRALIAN SOLDIER

Of English stock, but on Hellenic tree
Grafted, I fell in famed Thermopylae.

April 1941

AFTER THE GREEK

TOO LATE

Justice my ally; yet an unjust fate
Fell swift on me—my ally was too late.

BOMBED CITY

Our city, that should live to mourn us dead,
Dies, and we living gather round her bed.

CONVOY

Heed not my tomb, but sail. When we were gone,
The convoy, all the rest of it, held on.

THE BIAS

If there be some wild beauty worth
My love in every land on earth,
How claim impartial Nature yields
No riches but in English fields?—
> And yet forgive me if I hold it treason
> Not to love those fields past reason.

If some dark, festering homeland town
Call anger on its makers down,
How claim none but a foreign State
Has store of evil worth my hate?—
> And yet forgive me if I turn my anger,
> Fresh and whole, against the stranger.

Though love, when peace resumes, may roam
To tryst with beauty far from home,
And anger find its chiefest mark
In England, where some town lies dark—
> Yet still forgive me if my heart discover
> Proof that I am England's lover.

ENGLAND AGAIN IS OURS

England again is ours, to whom again
> We prodigal, we penitent, return
From husks of darkening Alp and deathly plain,
> Humble to find her faithful beauty burn

So memory-full, so passionate, so still,
> That we, who were in thrall to the immense,
End that apostasy, submit our will,
> Worship her smallness, love her difference.

Yet is she all of Europe: in this bound
    Of guarded freedom set with sounding waves
Are infinite hopes of anguished races found,
    The fervent prayers of men miscounted slaves.

ATLANTIC

No season frontiers here: the snow-white foam
    Expects no dark campaigning of the Spring;
No gold corn trampled; no long lived-in home
    Smoking in ruins, a tear-pictured thing.

Here bitter war has no such weeping; loss
    Is borne unseen, and gain goes unrenowned.
The convoy to safe harbour wins; no cross
    Marks where the ship was sunk, the sailor drowned.

TIMELESS

Deep sea is a terribly quiet place.
All is one night, and has no moon there;
Nor any familiar second to the minute,
Month to year.

Watches have ticked so long, he listening
Mistakes at once the quiet for mere peace;
Sinking through with closed eyes suddenly,
As the sounds cease.

SHOT AT DAWN

These watchers, whose prophetic sight
No darkness could withhold
From seeing and from hailing light,
Were shot at dawn, blindfold.

THE DOUBTERS

We slept in dream-paralysis who saw
Dancing over our heads the prairie fire,
Consuming crops and woods a crackle of straw;

Till nearer light cut into our lids like daybreak,
And over the dry summer fields of plenty
Was only the prosperous sun; this was to wake.

Now in the dream come true, the desolate land,
Our dreadful eyes are purged, the sun being darkened.
We stretch; our sinews loosen; we reach our hand,

And stubbing painful fingers down to the root
Of the slain pasture we, the unbelieving,
Astonished feel the stir of the green shoot.

www.ingramcontent.com/pod-product-compliance
Ingram Content Group UK Ltd.
Pitfield, Milton Keynes, MK11 3LW, UK
UKHW020448010325
455719UK00015B/477